SILENCE IN THE SNOWY FIELDS

Silence in the Snowy Fields

POEMS BY ROBERT BLY

Wesleyan University Press : MIDDLETOWN, CONNECTICUT

Library of Congress Catalog Card Number: 62–18340
Manufactured in the United States of America
First printing October 1962; second printing November 1963; third printing September 1964; fourth printing September 1966; fifth printing April 1967

"We are all asleep in the outward man."
— JACOB BOEHME

CONTENTS

Eleven Poems of Solitude

Awakening

Silence on the Roads

ELEVEN POEMS OF SOLITUDE

THREE KINDS OF PLEASURES

I

Sometimes, riding in a car, in Wisconsin
Or Illinois, you notice those dark telephone poles
One by one lift themselves out of the fence line
And slowly leap on the gray sky —
And past them, the snowy fields.

II

The darkness drifts down like snow on the picked cornfields
In Wisconsin: and on these black trees
Scattered, one by one,
Through the winter fields —
We see stiff weeds and brownish stubble,
And white snow left now only in the wheeltracks of the
    combine.

III

It is a pleasure, also, to be driving
Toward Chicago, near dark,
And see the lights in the barns.
The bare trees more dignified than ever,
Like a fierce man on his deathbed,
And the ditches along the road half full of a private snow.

RETURN TO SOLITUDE

I

It is a moonlit, windy night.
The moon has pushed out the Milky Way.
Clouds are hardly alive, and the grass leaping.
It is the hour of return.

II

We want to go back, to return to the sea,
The sea of solitary corridors,
And halls of wild nights,
Explosions of grief,
Diving into the sea of death,
Like the stars of the wheeling Bear.

III

What shall we find when we return?
Friends changed, houses moved,
Trees perhaps, with new leaves.

WAKING FROM SLEEP

Inside the veins there are navies setting forth,
Tiny explosions at the water lines,
And seagulls weaving in the wind of the salty blood.

It is the morning. The country has slept the whole winter.
Window seats were covered with fur skins, the yard was full
Of stiff dogs, and hands that clumsily held heavy books.

Now we wake, and rise from bed, and eat breakfast! —
Shouts rise from the harbor of the blood,
Mist, and masts rising, the knock of wooden tackle in the
    sunlight.

Now we sing, and do tiny dances on the kitchen floor.
Our whole body is like a harbor at dawn;
We know that our master has left us for the day.

HUNTING PHEASANTS IN A CORNFIELD

I

What is so strange about a tree alone in an open field?
It is a willow tree. I walk around and around it.
The body is strangely torn, and cannot leave it.
At last I sit down beneath it.

II

It is a willow tree alone in acres of dry corn.
Its leaves are scattered around its trunk, and around me,
Brown now, and speckled with delicate black.
Only the cornstalks now can make a noise.

III

The sun is cold, burning through the frosty distances of space.
The weeds are frozen to death long ago.
Why then do I love to watch
The sun moving on the chill skin of the branches?

IV

The mind has shed leaves alone for years.
It stands apart with small creatures near its roots.
I am happy in this ancient place,
A spot easily caught sight of above the corn,
If I were a young animal ready to turn home at dusk.

SURPRISED BY EVENING

There is unknown dust that is near us,
Waves breaking on shores just over the hill,
Trees full of birds that we have never seen,
Nets drawn down with dark fish.

The evening arrives; we look up and it is there,
It has come through the nets of the stars,
Through the tissues of the grass,
Walking quietly over the asylums of the waters.

The day shall never end, we think:
We have hair that seems born for the daylight;
But, at last, the quiet waters of the night will rise,
And our skin shall see far off, as it does under water.

THINKING OF WALLACE STEVENS
ON THE FIRST SNOWY DAY IN DECEMBER

This new snow seems to speak of virgins
With frail clothes made of gold,
Just as the old snow shall whisper
Of concierges in France.

The new dawn sings of beaches
Dazzling as sugar and clean as the clouds of Greece,
Just as the exhausted dusk shall sing
Of the waves on the western shore.

This new strength whispers of the darkness of death,
Of the frail skiff lost in the giant cave,
Just as in the boat nearing death you sang
Of feathers and white snow.

SUNSET AT A LAKE

The sun is sinking. Here on the pine-haunted bank, the mosquitoes fly around drowsily, and moss stands out as if it wanted to speak. Calm falls on the lake, which now seems heavier and inhospitable. Far out, rafts of ducks drift like closed eyes, and a thin line of silver caused by something invisible slowly moves toward shore in the viscous darkness under the southern bank. Only a few birds, the troubled ones, speak to the darkening roof of earth; small weeds stand abandoned, the clay is sending her gifts back to the center of the earth.

Because it is the first Sunday of pheasant season, men gather in the lights of cars to divide pheasants, and the chickens, huddling near their electricity, and in some slight fear of the dark, walk for the last time about their little hut, whose floor seems now so bare.

The dusk has come, a glow in the west, as if seen through the isinglass on old coal stoves, and the cows stand around the barn door; now the farmer looks up at the paling sky reminding him of death, and in the fields the bones of the corn rustle faintly in the last wind, and the half moon stands in the south.

Now the lights from barn windows can be seen through bare trees.

APPROACHING WINTER

I

September. Clouds. The first day for wearing jackets.
The corn is wandering in dark corridors,
Near the well and the whisper of tombs.

II

I sit alone surrounded by dry corn,
Near the second growth of the pigweeds,
And hear the corn leaves scrape their feet on the wind.

III

Fallen ears are lying on the dusty earth.
The useful ears will lie dry in cribs, but the others, missed
By the picker, will lie here touching the ground the whole
    winter.

IV

Snow will come, and cover the husks of the fallen ears
With flakes infinitely delicate, like jewels of a murdered
    Gothic prince
Which were lost centuries ago during a great battle.

DRIVING TOWARD
THE LAC QUI PARLE RIVER

I

I am driving; it is dusk; Minnesota.
The stubble field catches the last growth of sun.
The soybeans are breathing on all sides.
Old men are sitting before their houses on carseats
In the small towns. I am happy,
The moon rising above the turkey sheds.

II

The small world of the car
Plunges through the deep fields of the night,
On the road from Willmar to Milan.
This solitude covered with iron
Moves through the fields of night
Penetrated by the noise of crickets.

III

Nearly to Milan, suddenly a small bridge,
And water kneeling in the moonlight.
In small towns the houses are built right on the ground;
The lamplight falls on all fours in the grass.
When I reach the river, the full moon covers it;
A few people are talking low in a boat.

POEM IN THREE PARTS

I

Oh, on an early morning I think I shall live forever!
I am wrapped in my joyful flesh,
As the grass is wrapped in its clouds of green.

II

Rising from a bed, where I dreamt
Of long rides past castles and hot coals,
The sun lies happily on my knees;
I have suffered and survived the night
Bathed in dark water, like any blade of grass.

III

The strong leaves of the box-elder tree,
Plunging in the wind, call us to disappear
Into the wilds of the universe,
Where we shall sit at the foot of a plant,
And live forever, like the dust.

AWAKENING

UNREST

A strange unrest hovers over the nation:
This is the last dance, the wild tossing of Morgan's seas,
The division of spoils. A lassitude
Enters into the diamonds of the body.
In high school the explosion begins, the child is partly killed,
When the fight is over, and the land and the sea ruined,
Two shapes inside us rise, and move away.

But the baboon whistles on the shores of death —
Climbing and falling, tossing nuts and stones,
He gambols by the tree
Whose branches hold the expanses of cold,
The planets whirling and the black sun,
The cries of insects, and the tiny slaves
In the prisons of bark:
Charlemagne, we are approaching your islands!

We are returning now to the snowy trees,
And the depth of the darkness buried in snow, through
    which you rode all night
With stiff hands; now the darkness is falling
In which we sleep and awake — a darkness in which
Thieves shudder, and the insane have a hunger for snow,
In which bankers dream of being buried by black stones,
And businessmen fall on their knees in the dungeons of
    sleep.

AWAKENING

We are approaching sleep: the chestnut blossoms in the
    mind
Mingle with thoughts of pain
And the long roots of barley, bitterness
As of the oak roots staining the waters dark
In Louisiana, the wet streets soaked with rain
And sodden blossoms, out of this
We have come, a tunnel softly hurtling into darkness.

The storm is coming. The small farmhouse in Minnesota
Is hardly strong enough for the storm.
Darkness, darkness in grass, darkness in trees.
Even the water in wells trembles.
Bodies give off darkness, and chrysanthemums
Are dark, and horses, who are bearing great loads of hay
To the deep barns where the dark air is moving from
    corners.

Lincoln's statue, and the traffic. From the long past
Into the long present
A bird, forgotten in these pressures, warbling,
As the great wheel turns around, grinding
The living in water.
Washing, continual washing, in water now stained
With blossoms and rotting logs,
Cries, half-muffled, from beneath the earth, the living
    awakened at last like the dead.

POEM AGAINST THE RICH

Each day I live, each day the sea of light
Rises, I seem to see
The tear inside the stone
As if my eyes were gazing beneath the earth.
The rich man in his red hat
Cannot hear
The weeping in the pueblos of the lily,
Or the dark tears in the shacks of the corn.
Each day the sea of light rises
I hear the sad rustle of the darkened armies,
Where each man weeps, and the plaintive
Orisons of the stones.
The stones bow as the saddened armies pass.

POEM AGAINST THE BRITISH

I

The wind through the box-elder trees
Is like rides at dusk on a white horse,
Wars for your country, and fighting the British.

II

I wonder if Washington listened to the trees.
All morning I have been sitting in grass,
Higher than my eyes, beneath trees,
And listening upward, to the wind in leaves.
Suddenly I realize there is one thing more:
There is also the wind through the high grass.

III

There are palaces, boats, silence among white buildings,
Iced drinks on marble tops, among cool rooms;
It is good also to be poor, and listen to the wind.

The dove returns: it found no resting place;
It was in flight all night above the shaken seas;
Beneath ark eaves
The dove shall magnify the tiger's bed;
Give the dove peace.
The split-tail swallows leave the sill at dawn;
At dusk, blue swallows shall return.
On the third day the crow shall fly;
The crow, the crow, the spider-colored crow,
The crow shall find new mud to walk upon.

REMEMBERING IN OSLO THE OLD PICTURE
OF THE MAGNA CARTA

The girl in a house dress, pushing open the window,
Is also the fat king sitting under the oak tree,
And the garbage men, thumping their cans, are
Crows still cawing,
And the nobles are offering the sheet to the king.
One thing is also another thing, and the doomed galleons,
Hung with trinkets, hove by the coast, and in the blossoms
Of trees are still sailing on their long voyage from Spain;
I too am still shocking grain, as I did as a boy, dog tired,
And my great-grandfather steps on his ship.

SUMMER, 1960, MINNESOTA

I

After a drifting day, visiting the bridge near Louisberg,
With its hot muddy water flowing
Under the excited swallows,
Now, at noon
We plunge through the hot beanfields,
And the sturdy alfalfa fields, the farm groves
Like heavy green smoke close to the ground.

II

Inside me there is a confusion of swallows,
Birds flying through the smoke,
And horses galloping excitedly on fields of short grass.

III

Yet, we are falling,
Falling into the open mouths of darkness,
Into the Congo as if into a river,
Or as wheat into open mills.

With pale women in Maryland,
Passing the proud and tragic pastures,
And stupefied with love
And the stupendous burdens of the foreign trees,
As all before us lived, dazed
With overabundant love in the reach of the Chesapeake,
Past the tobacco warehouse, through our dark lives
Like those before, we move to the death we love
With pale women in Maryland.

DRIVING THROUGH OHIO

I

We slept that night in Delaware, Ohio:
A magnificent and sleepy country,
Oak country, sheep country, sod country.
We slept in a huge white tourist home
With *National Geographics* on the table.

II

North of Columbus there is a sort of torpid joy:
The slow and muddy river,
The white barns leaning into the ground,
Cottonwoods with their trunks painted white,
And houses with small observatories on top,
As if Ohio were the widow's coast, looking over
The dangerous Atlantic.

III

Now we drive north past the white cemeteries
So rich in the morning air!
All morning I have felt the sense of death;
I am full of love, and love this torpid land.
Some day I will go back, and inhabit again
The sleepy ground where Harding was born.

I

Here we are, all dressed up to honor death!
No, it is not that;
It is to honor this old woman
Born in Bellingham.

II

The church windows are open to the green trees.
The minister tells us that, being
The sons and daughters of God,
We rejoice at death, for we go
To the mansions prepared
From the foundations of the world.
Impossible. No one believes it.

III

Out on the bare, pioneer field,
The frail body must wait till dusk
To be lowered
In the hot and sandy earth.

ON THE FERRY ACROSS CHESAPEAKE BAY

On the orchard of the sea, far out are whitecaps,
Water that answers questions no one has asked,
Silent speakers of the grave's rejoinders;
Having accomplished nothing, I am travelling somewhere
      else;
O deep green sea, it is not for you
This smoking body ploughs toward death;
It is not for the strange blossoms of the sea
I drag my thin legs across the Chesapeake Bay;
Though perhaps by your motions the body heals;
For though on its road the body cannot march
With golden trumpets — it must march —
And the sea gives up its answer as it falls into itself.

What cave are you in, hiding, rained on?
Like a wife, starving, without care,
Water dripping from your head, bent
Over ground corn . . .

    You raise your face into the rain
That drives over the valley —
Forgive me, your husband,
On the streets of a distant city, laughing,
With many appointments,
Though at night going also
To a bare room, a room of poverty,
To sleep among a bare pitcher and basin
In a room with no heat —

    Which of us two then is the worse off?
And how did this separation come about?

DEPRESSION

I felt my heart beat like an engine high in the air,
Like those scaffolding engines standing only on planks;
My body hung about me like an old grain elevator,
Useless, clogged, full of blackened wheat.
My body was sour, my life dishonest, and I fell asleep.

I dreamt that men came toward me, carrying thin wires;
I felt the wires pass in, like fire; they were old Tibetans,
Dressed in padded clothes, to keep out cold;
Then three work gloves, lying fingers to fingers,
In a circle, came toward me, and I awoke.

Now I want to go back among the dark roots;
Now I want to see the day pulling its long wing;
I want to see nothing more than two feet high;
I want to see no one, I want to say nothing,
I want to go down and rest in the black earth of silence.

DRIVING TO TOWN LATE TO MAIL A LETTER

It is a cold and snowy night. The main street is deserted.
The only things moving are swirls of snow.
As I lift the mailbox door, I feel its cold iron.
There is a privacy I love in this snowy night.
Driving around, I will waste more time.

GETTING UP EARLY

I am up early. The box-elder leaves have fallen.
The eastern sky is the color of March.
The sky has spread out over the world like water.
The bootlegger and his wife are still asleep.

I saw the light first from the barn well.
The cold water fell into the night-chilled buckets,
Deepening to the somber blue of the southern sky.
Over the new trees, there was a strange light in the east.

The light was dawn. Like a man who has come home
After seeing many dark rivers, and will soon go again,
The dawn stood there with a quiet gaze;
Our eyes met through the top leaves of the young ash.

Dawn has come. The clouds floating in the east have turned
      white.
The fence posts have stopped being a part of the darkness.
The depth has disappeared from the puddles on the ground.
I look up angrily at the light.

A silence hovers over the earth:
The grass lifts lightly in the heat
Like the ancient wing of a bird.
A horse gazes steadily at me.

LOVE POEM

When we are in love, we love the grass,
And the barns, and the lightpoles,
And the small mainstreets abandoned all night.

"TAKING THE HANDS"

Taking the hands of someone you love,
You see they are delicate cages . . .
Tiny birds are singing
In the secluded prairies
And in the deep valleys of the hand.

AFTERNOON SLEEP

I

I was descending from the mountains of sleep.
Asleep I had gazed east over a sunny field,
And sat on the running board of an old Model A.
I awoke happy, for I had dreamt of my wife,
And the loneliness hiding in grass and weeds
That lies near a man over thirty, and suddenly enters.

II

When Joe Sjolie grew tired, he sold his farm,
Even his bachelor rocker, and did not come back.
He left his dog behind in the cob shed.
The dog refused to take food from strangers.

III

I drove out to that farm when I awoke;
Alone on a hill, sheltered by trees.
The matted grass lay around the house.
When I climbed the porch, the door was open.
Inside were old abandoned books,
And instructions to Norwegian immigrants.

43

IMAGES SUGGESTED BY MEDIEVAL MUSIC

For Margaret and Joseph Scheinin

"A thousand singing herons I saw passing
Flying overhead, sounding a thousand voices
Exulting: Glory be in the heaven, etc."

I

Once more in Brooklyn Heights
A child is born, and it has no father,
And it is right to rejoice: our past life appears
As a wake behind us, and we plunge on into the sea of pain.

II

I have felt this joy before, it is like the harsh grasses
On lonely beaches, this strange sweetness
Of medieval music, a hoarse joy,
Like birds', or the joy of trackless seas,
Columbus' ships covered with ice,
Palace children dancing among finely worked gold:

III

As I listen, I am a ship, skirting
A thousand harbors, as once, sailing off the coast of Crete,
And turning in, we will find the steep climb from the
    harbor;
The voyage goes on. The joy of sailing and the open sea!

SOLITUDE LATE AT NIGHT IN THE WOODS

I

The body is like a November birch facing the full moon
And reaching into the cold heavens.
In these trees there is no ambition, no sodden body, no
    leaves,
Nothing but bare trunks climbing like cold fire!

II

My last walk in the trees has come. At dawn
I must return to the trapped fields,
To the obedient earth.
The trees shall be reaching all the winter.

III

It is a joy to walk in the bare woods.
The moonlight is not broken by the heavy leaves.
The leaves are down, and touching the soaked earth,
Giving off the odor that partridges love.

How strange to think of giving up all ambition!
Suddenly I see with such clear eyes
The white flake of snow
That has just fallen in the horse's mane!

IN A TRAIN

There has been a light snow.
Dark car tracks move in out of the darkness.
I stare at the train window marked with soft dust.
I have awakened at Missoula, Montana, utterly happy.

SILENCE ON THE ROADS

AFTER WORKING

I

After many strange thoughts,
Thoughts of distant harbors, and new life,
I came in and found the moonlight lying in the room.

II

Outside it covers the trees like pure sound,
The sound of tower bells, or of water moving under the ice,
The sound of the deaf hearing through the bones
    of their heads.

III

We know the road; as the moonlight
Lifts everything, so in a night like this
The road goes on ahead, it is all clear.

I can see outside the gold wings without birds
Flying around, and the wells of cold water
Without walls standing eighty feet up in the air,
I can feel the crickets' singing carrying them into the sky.

I know these cold shadows are falling for hundreds of miles,
Crossing lawns in tiny towns, and the doors of Catholic
    churches;
I know the horse of darkness is riding fast to the east,
Carrying a thin man with no coat.

And I know the sun is sinking down great stairs,
Like an executioner with a great blade walking into a cellar,
And the gold animals, the lions, and the zebras, and the
    pheasants,
Are waiting at the head of the stairs with robbers' eyes.

LAZINESS AND SILENCE

I

On a Saturday afternoon in the football season,
I lie in a bed near the lake,
And dream of moles with golden wings.

While the depth of the water trembles on the ceiling,
Like the tail of an enraged bird,
I watch the dust floating above the bed, content.

I think of ships leaving lonely harbors,
Dolphins playing far at sea,
Fish with the faces of old men come in from a blizzard.

II

A dream of moles with golden wings
Is not so bad; it is like imagining
Waterfalls of stone deep in mountains,
Or a wing flying alone beneath the earth.

I know that far out in the Minnesota lake
Fish are nosing the mouths of cold springs,
Whose water causes ripples in the sleeping sand,
Like a spirit moving in a body.

It is Saturday afternoon. Crowds are gathered,
Warmed by the sun, and the pure air.
I thought of this strange mole this morning,
After sleeping all night by the lake.

53

I

Tonight I rode through the cornfield in the moonlight!
The dying grass is still, waiting for winter,
And the dark weeds are waiting, as if under water . . .

II

In Arabia, the horses live in the tents,
Near dark gold, and water, and tombs.

III

How beautiful to walk out at midnight in the moonlight
Dreaming of animals.

NIGHT

I

If I think of a horse wandering about sleeplessly
All night on this short grass covered with moonlight,
I feel a joy, as if I had thought
Of a pirate ship ploughing through dark flowers.

II

The box elders around us are full of joy,
Obeying what is beneath them.
The lilacs are sleeping, and the plants are sleeping,
Even the wood made into a casket is asleep.

III

The butterfly is carrying loam on his wings;
The toad is bearing tiny bits of granite in his skin;
The leaves at the crown of the tree are asleep
Like the dark bits of earth at its root.

IV

Alive, we are like a sleek black water beetle,
Skating across still water in any direction
We choose, and soon to be swallowed
Suddenly from beneath.

AFTER DRINKING ALL NIGHT WITH A FRIEND, WE GO OUT IN A BOAT AT DAWN TO SEE WHO CAN WRITE THE BEST POEM

These pines, these fall oaks, these rocks,
This water dark and touched by wind —
I am like you, you dark boat,
Drifting over water fed by cool springs.

Beneath the waters, since I was a boy,
I have dreamt of strange and dark treasures,
Not of gold, or strange stones, but the true
Gift, beneath the pale lakes of Minnesota.

This morning also, drifting in the dawn wind,
I sense my hands, and my shoes, and this ink —
Drifting, as all of this body drifts,
Above the clouds of the flesh and the stone.

A few friendships, a few dawns, a few glimpses of grass,
A few oars weathered by the snow and the heat,
So we drift toward shore, over cold waters,
No longer caring if we drift or go straight.

OLD BOARDS

I

I love to see boards lying on the ground in early spring:
The ground beneath them is wet, and muddy —
Perhaps covered with chicken tracks —
And they are dry and eternal.

II

This is the wood one sees on the decks of ocean ships,
Wood that carries us far from land,
With a dryness of something used for simple tasks,
Like a horse's tail.

III

This wood is like a man who has a simple life,
Living through the spring and winter on the ship of his own
    desire.
He sits on dry wood surrounded by half-melted snow
As the rooster walks away springily over the dampened hay.

LATE AT NIGHT
DURING A VISIT OF FRIENDS

I

We spent all day fishing and talking.
At last, late at night, I sit at my desk alone,
And rise and walk out in the summery night.
A dark thing hopped near me in the grass.

II

The trees were breathing, the windmill slowly pumped.
Overhead the rain clouds that rained on Ortonville
Covered half the stars.
The air was still cool from their rain.

III

It is very late.
I am the only one awake.
Men and women I love are sleeping nearby.

IV

The human face shines as it speaks of things
Near itself, thoughts full of dreams.
The human face shines like a dark sky
As it speaks of those things that oppress the living.

SILENCE

The fall has come, clear as the eyes of chickens.
Strange muffled sounds come from the sea,
Sounds of muffled oarlocks,
And swampings in lonely bays,
Surf crashing on unchristened shores,
And the wash of tiny snail shells in the wandering gravel.

My body also wanders among these doorposts and cars,
Cradling a pen, or walking down a stair
Holding a cup in my hand,
And not breaking into the pastures that lie in the sunlight.
This is the sloth of the man inside the body,
The sloth of the body lost among the wandering stones of
    kindness.

Something homeless is looking on the long roads —
A dog lost since midnight, a small duck
Among the odorous reeds,
Or a tiny box-elder bug searching for the window pane.
Even the young sunlight is lost on the window pane,
Moving at night like a diver among the bare branches
    silently lying on the floor.

SNOWFALL IN THE AFTERNOON

I

The grass is half-covered with snow.
It was the sort of snowfall that starts in late afternoon,
And now the little houses of the grass are growing dark.

II

If I reached my hands down, near the earth,
I could take handfuls of darkness!
A darkness was always there, which we never noticed.

III

As the snow grows heavier, the cornstalks fade farther away,
And the barn moves nearer to the house.
The barn moves all alone in the growing storm.

IV

The barn is full of corn, and moving toward us now,
Like a hulk blown toward us in a storm at sea;
All the sailors on deck have been blind for many years.

Distinguished contemporary poetry in cloth and paperback editions

ALAN ANSEN: *Disorderly Houses* (1961)

JOHN ASHBERY: *The Tennis Court Oath* (1962)

ROBERT BAGG: *Madonna of the Cello* (1961)

ROBERT BLY: *Silence in the Snowy Fields* (1962)

TURNER CASSITY: *Watchboy, What of the Night?* (1966)

TRAM COMBS: *st. thomas. poems.* (1965)

DONALD DAVIE: *Events and Wisdoms* (1965); *New and Selected Poems* (1961)

JAMES DICKEY: *Buckdancer's Choice* (1965) [National Book Award in Poetry, 1966]; *Drowning With Others* (1962); *Helmets* (1964)

DAVID FERRY: *On the Way to the Island* (1960)

ROBERT FRANCIS: *The Orb Weaver* (1960)

JOHN HAINES: *Winter News* (1966)

RICHARD HOWARD: *Quantities* (1962)

BARBARA HOWES: *Light and Dark* (1959)

DAVID IGNATOW: *Figures of the Human* (1964); *Say Pardon* (1961)

DONALD JUSTICE: *The Summer Anniversaries* (1960); [A Lamont Poetry Selection]

CHESTER KALLMAN: *Absent and Present* (1963)

VASSAR MILLER: *My Bones Being Wiser* (1963); *Wage War on Silence* (1960)

W. R. MOSES: *Identities* (1965)

DONALD PETERSEN: *The Spectral Boy* (1964)

HYAM PLUTZIK: *Apples from Shinar* (1959)

VERN RUTSALA: *The Window* (1964)

HARVEY SHAPIRO: *Battle Report* (1966)

JON SILKIN: *Poems New and Selected* (1966)

LOUIS SIMPSON: *At the End of the Open Road* (1963) [Pulitzer Prize in Poetry, 1964]; *A Dream of Governors* (1959)

JAMES WRIGHT: *The Branch Will Not Break* (1963); *Saint Judas* (1959)